MIGHTY MOVERS

Earth Movers

A Buddy Book

by

Sarah Tieck

ABDO
Publishing Company

VISIT US AT
www.abdopub.com

Published by ABDO Publishing Company, 4940 Viking Drive, Edina, Minnesota 55435.

Printed in the United States.

Written and Edited by: Sarah Tieck
Contributing Editor: Michael P. Goecke
Graphic Design: Maria Hosley
Image Research: Sarah Tieck
Photographs: Michael P. Goecke, Photos.com
Special thanks to Schlomka Excavating, Inc.

Library of Congress Cataloging-in-Publication Data

Tieck, Sarah, 1976-
  Earthmovers / Sarah Tieck.
      p. cm. — (Mighty movers)
  ISBN 1-59197-826-2
    1. Earthmmoving machinery—Juvenile literature. I. Title.

TA725.T53 2004
629.225—dc22

                                                    2004050236

Table of Contents

What Are Earth Movers?

Earth movers are building machines. Scrapers, bulldozers, and excavators are earth movers. Earth movers help get land ready for building. They also help move dirt from one place to another.

Excavators scoop rocks and dirt.

What Do Earth Movers Do?

Earth movers work at construction sites. They help get land ready for building.

Some building machines clear trees and rocks from the land. Earth movers also move dirt. This makes the land flat. When the land is flat, the crew can start building.

Workers build houses and buildings at construction sites.

Scrapers

A scraper is an earth mover. A scraper uses a **blade** to move dirt. The blade is dragged over the ground. This puts dirt into a big bin. The bin fills with dirt as the scraper moves. When the scraper's bin is full, the dirt is emptied to where it is needed.

The scraper's bin is called a can.

Bulldozers

A bulldozer is an earth mover. A bulldozer also has a blade on its front. Its blade pushes dirt to smooth the land. A bulldozer has a part called a ripper on its back. The ripper looks like a giant rake. It helps move rocks. The ripper also helps break up rough land.

The bulldozer's blade pushes dirt.

Farmers use a bulldozer's blade
to do farmwork.

A bulldozer moves rocks to get land
ready for building.

Excavators

An excavator is an earth mover. An excavator digs holes using a bucket. The bucket has sharp parts to help break up hard ground. The bucket lifts rocks and dirt.

The excavator's bucket is like a shovel.

The bucket scoops up mud and rocks.

The excavator has parts that move.

How Earth Movers Work

An earth mover's parts work because of something called hydraulics. Hydraulics is the use of liquids such as water and oil to move machines. Pressure created by the liquid makes the machine's parts move. Hydraulics help earth movers move dirt.

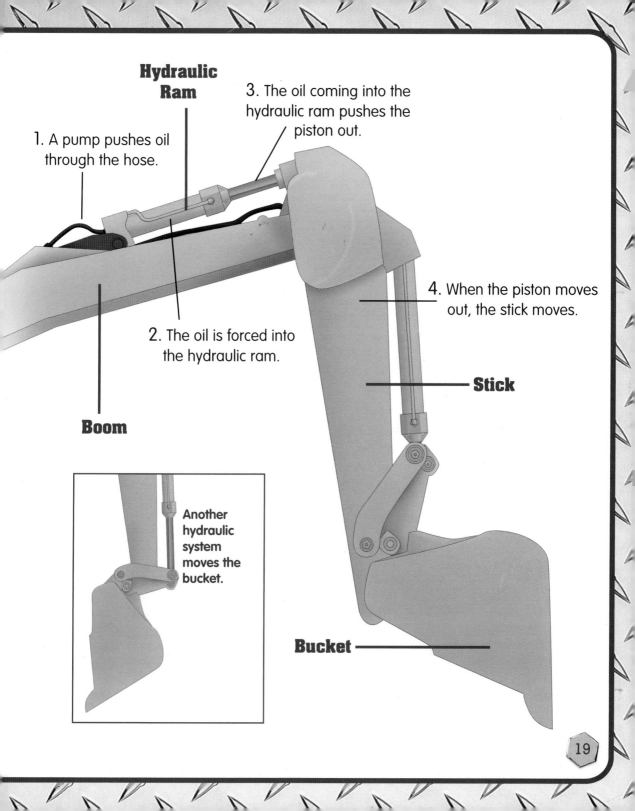

Hydraulic Ram

3. The oil coming into the hydraulic ram pushes the piston out.

1. A pump pushes oil through the hose.

4. When the piston moves out, the stick moves.

2. The oil is forced into the hydraulic ram.

Stick

Boom

Another hydraulic system moves the bucket.

Bucket

The earth mover's driver is called an operator. The operator rides in the earth mover's cab. The cab is made to be safe for the operator.

Each earth mover's controls are in its cab. The operator turns the earth mover using a steering wheel. The operator moves levers, too. Levers make the earth mover's parts work.

Levers help control the earth mover.

Other Jobs Earth Movers Do

Most often, earth movers work on construction sites. But, earth movers do other things. Earth movers can help fill big holes with dirt. They can help crews make roads. Earth movers can help clear land for new parks, too.

Earth movers help clean up trees to make space for parks.

Important Words

blade a metal tool that is part of an earth mover. The blade works like a shovel to push dirt.

construction site the place where a house or building is built.

crew a group of people who work together.

hydraulics the force of liquid, which is used to make machines move.

levers a bar that the operator moves to make the machine move.

operator the crew member who operates a building machine.

Web Sites

To learn more about earth movers, visit ABDO Publishing Company on the World Wide Web. Web site links about earth movers are featured on our Book Links page. These links are routinely monitored and updated to provide the most current information available.

www.abdopub.com

Index